Wedding Planner
Mr ♥ Mrs

Wedding Planner...

♡

WEDDING DATE & TIME:

TO DO LIST:

VENUE ADDRESS:

BUDGET:

OFFICIANT:

WEDDING PARTY:

NOTES & REMINDERS:

Wedding Budget...

	TOTAL COST:	DEPOSIT:	REMAINDER:
WEDDING VENUE			
RECEPTION VENUE			
FLORIST			
OFFICIANT			
CATERER			
WEDDING CAKE			
BRIDAL ATTIRE			
GROOM ATTIRE			
BRIDAL JEWELRY			
BRIDESMAID ATTIRE			
GROOMSMEN ATTIRE			
HAIR & MAKE UP			
PHOTOGRAPHER			
VIDEOGRAPHER			
DJ SERVICE/ENTERTAINMENT			
INVITATIONS			
TRANSPORTATION			
WEDDING PARTY GIFTS			
RENTALS			
HONEYMOON			

12 Months Before...

SET THE DATE

SET YOUR BUDGET

CHOOSE YOUR THEME

ORGANIZE ENGAGEMENT PARTY

RESEARCH VENUES

BOOK A WEDDING PLANNER

RESEARCH PHOTOGRAPHERS

RESEARCH VIDEOGRAPHERS

RESEARCH DJ'S/ENTERTAINMENT

CONSIDER FLORISTS

RESEARCH CATERERS

DECIDE ON OFFICIANT

CREATE INITIAL GUEST LIST

CHOOSE WEDDING PARTY

SHOP FOR WEDDING DRESS

REGISTER WITH GIFT REGISTRY

DISCUSS HONEYMOON IDEAS

RESEARCH WEDDING RINGS

THINGS TO REMEMBER:

9 Months Before...

FINALIZE GUEST LIST

ORDER INVITATIONS

PLAN YOUR RECEPTION

BOOK PHOTOGRAPHER

BOOK VIDEOGRAPHER

BOOK FLORIST

BOOK DJ/ENTERTAINMENT

BOOK CATERER

CHOOSE WEDDING CAKE

CHOOSE WEDDING GOWN

ORDER BRIDESMAIDS DRESSES

RESERVE TUXEDOS

ARRANGE TRANSPORTATION

BOOK WEDDING VENUE

BOOK RECEPTION VENUE

PLAN HONEYMOON

BOOK OFFICIANT

BOOK ROOMS FOR GUESTS

THINGS TO REMEMBER:

6 Months Before...

ORDER THANK YOU NOTES

REVIEW RECEPTION DETAILS

MAKE APPT FOR DRESS FITTING

CONFIRM BRIDEMAIDS DRESSES

GET MARRIAGE LICENSE

BOOK HAIR/MAKE UP STYLIST

CONFIRM MUSIC SELECTIONS

PLAN BRIDAL SHOWER

PLAN REHEARSAL

SHOP FOR WEDDING RINGS

THINGS TO REMEMBER:

3 Months Before...

MAIL OUT INVITATIONS

MEET WITH OFFICIANT

BUY GIFTS FOR WEDDING PARTY

BOOK FINAL GOWN FITTING

BUY WEDDING BANDS

PLAN YOUR HAIR STYLE

PURCHASE SHOES/HEELS

CONFIRM PASSPORTS ARE VALID

FINALIZE RECEPTION MENU

PLAN REHEARSAL DINNER

CONFIRM ALL BOOKINGS

APPLY FOR MARRIAGE LICENSE

CONFIRM MUSIC SELECTIONS

DRAFT WEDDING VOWS

CHOOSE YOUR MC

ARRANGE AIRPORT TRANSFER

THINGS TO REMEMBER:

1 Month Before...

CONFIRM FINAL GUEST COUNT

CONFIRM RECEPTION DETAILS

ATTEND FINAL GOWN FITTING

CONFIRM PHOTOGRAPHER

WRAP WEDDING PARTY GIFTS

CREATE PHOTOGRAPHY SHOT LIST

REHEARSE WEDDING VOWS

BOOK MANI-PEDI

CONFIRM WITH FLORIST

CONFIRM VIDEOGRAPHER

PICK UP BRIDEMAIDS DRESSES

CREATE WEDDING SCHEDULE

THINGS TO REMEMBER:

1 Week Before...

FINALIZE SEATING PLANS

MAKE PAYMENTS TO VENDORS

PACK FOR HONEYMOON

CONFIRM HOTEL RESERVATIONS

GIVE SCHEDULE TO PARTY

DELIVER LICENSE TO OFFICIANT

CONFIRM WITH BAKERY

PICK UP WEDDING DRESS

PICK UP TUXEDOS

GIVE MUSIC LIST TO DJ

THINGS TO REMEMBER:

The Day Before...

GET MANICURE/PEDICURE

ATTEND REHEARSAL DINNER

GET A GOOD NIGHT'S SLEEP!

GIVE GIFTS TO WEDDING PARTY

FINALIZE PACKING

TO DO LIST:

Wedding Planner...

ENGAGEMENT PARTY:

DATE:

LOCATION:

TIME:

NUMBER OF GUESTS:

NOTES:

BRIDAL SHOWER:

DATE:

LOCATION:

TIME:

NUMBER OF GUESTS:

NOTES:

STAG & DOE PARTY:

DATE:

LOCATION:

TIME:

NUMBER OF GUESTS:

NOTES:

Wedding Party

MAID/MATRON OF HONOR:

PHONE: _____   DRESS SIZE: _____   SHOE SIZE: _____

EMAIL: _____

BRIDESMAID:

PHONE: _____   DRESS SIZE: _____   SHOE SIZE: _____

EMAIL: _____

BRIDESMAID #2:

PHONE: _____   DRESS SIZE: _____   SHOE SIZE: _____

EMAIL: _____

BRIDESMAID #3:

PHONE: _____   DRESS SIZE: _____   SHOE SIZE: _____

EMAIL: _____

BRIDESMAID #4:

PHONE: _____   DRESS SIZE: _____   SHOE SIZE: _____

EMAIL: _____

Wedding Party

BEST MAN:

PHONE: WAIST SIZE: SHOE SIZE:

NECK SIZE: SLEEVE SIZE: JACKET SIZE:

EMAIL:

GROOMSMEN #1:

PHONE: WAIST SIZE: SHOE SIZE:

NECK SIZE: SLEEVE SIZE: JACKET SIZE:

EMAIL:

GROOMSMEN #2:

PHONE: WAIST SIZE: SHOE SIZE:

NECK SIZE: SLEEVE SIZE: JACKET SIZE:

EMAIL:

GROOMSMEN #3:

PHONE: WAIST SIZE: SHOE SIZE:

NECK SIZE: SLEEVE SIZE: JACKET SIZE:

EMAIL:

GROOMSMEN #4:

PHONE: WAIST SIZE: SHOE SIZE:

NECK SIZE: SLEEVE SIZE: JACKET SIZE:

EMAIL:

Photographer

PHOTOGRAPHER:

PHONE: _____   COMPANY: _____

EMAIL: _____   ADDRESS: _____

WEDDING PACKAGE OVERVIEW:

EST PRICE: _____

INCLUSIONS: YES ✓   NO ✓   COST:

ENGAGEMENT SHOOT: _____

PHOTO ALBUMS: _____

FRAMES: _____

PROOFS INCLUDED: _____

NEGATIVES INCLUDED: _____

TOTAL COST:

Videographer

VIDEOGRAPHER:

PHONE: COMPANY:

EMAIL: ADDRESS:

WEDDING PACKAGE OVERVIEW:

EST PRICE:

INCLUSIONS: YES ✓   NO ✓   COST:

DUPLICATES/COPIES:

PHOTO MONTAGE:

MUSIC ADDED:

EDITING:

TOTAL COST:

DJ/Entertainment

DJ/LIVE BAND/ENTERTAINMENT:

PHONE: _____   COMPANY: _____

EMAIL: _____   ADDRESS: _____

START TIME: _____   END TIME: _____

ENTERTAINMENT SERVICE OVERVIEW:

EST PRICE: _____

INCLUSIONS: YES ✓   NO ✓   COST: _____

 SOUND EQUIPMENT: _____

 LIGHTING: _____

 SPECIAL EFFECTS: _____

GRATUITIES

TOTAL COST: _____

Florist Planner

FLORIST:

PHONE: COMPANY:

EMAIL: ADDRESS:

FLORAL PACKAGE:

EST PRICE: _____

INCLUSIONS: YES ✓   NO ✓   COST:

BRIDAL BOUQUET:

THROW AWAY BOUQUET:

CORSAGES:

CEREMONY FLOWERS

CENTERPIECES

CAKE TOPPER

BOUTONNIERE

TOTAL COST:

Wedding Cake

PHONE: _____   COMPANY: _____

EMAIL: _____   ADDRESS: _____

WEDDING CAKE PACKAGE:

♡

COST: _____   FREE TASTING: _____   DELIVERY FEE: _____

FLAVOR: _____

FILLING: _____

SIZE: _____

SHAPE: _____

COLOR: _____

EXTRAS: _____

TOTAL COST:

Transportation Planner

TO CEREMONY: PICK UP TIME: PICK UP LOCATION:

BRIDE:

GROOM:

BRIDE'S PARENTS:

GROOM'S PARENTS:

BRIDESMAIDS:

GROOMSMEN:

NOTES:

TO RECEPTION: PICK UP TIME: PICK UP LOCATION:

BRIDE & GROOM:

BRIDE'S PARENTS:

GROOM'S PARENTS:

BRIDESMAIDS:

GROOMSMEN:

Wedding Planner...

BACHELORETTE PARTY:

DATE: _____   LOCATION: _____

TIME: _____   NUMBER OF GUESTS: _____

NOTES:

BACHELOR PARTY:

DATE: _____   LOCATION: _____

TIME: _____   NUMBER OF GUESTS: _____

NOTES:

CEREMONY REHEARSAL:

DATE: _____   LOCATION: _____

TIME: _____   NUMBER OF GUESTS: _____

NOTES:

Wedding Planner...

REHEARSAL DINNER:

DATE: LOCATION:

TIME: NUMBER OF GUESTS:

NOTES:

RECEPTION:

DATE: LOCATION:

TIME: NUMBER OF GUESTS:

NOTES:

REMINDERS:

Names & Addresses

CEREMONY:

PHONE: _____   CONTACT NAME: _____

EMAIL: _____   ADDRESS: _____

RECEPTION:

PHONE: _____   CONTACT NAME: _____

EMAIL: _____   ADDRESS: _____

OFFICIANT:

PHONE: _____   CONTACT NAME: _____

EMAIL: _____   ADDRESS: _____

WEDDING PLANNER:

PHONE: _____   CONTACT NAME: _____

EMAIL: _____   ADDRESS: _____

Names & Addresses

CATERER:

PHONE:

EMAIL:

CONTACT NAME:

ADDRESS:

FLORIST:

PHONE:

EMAIL:

CONTACT NAME:

ADDRESS:

BAKERY:

PHONE:

EMAIL:

CONTACT NAME:

ADDRESS:

BRIDAL SHOP:

PHONE:

EMAIL:

CONTACT NAME:

ADDRESS:

Names & Addresses

PHOTOGRAPHER:

PHONE: CONTACT NAME:

EMAIL: ADDRESS:

VIDEOGRAPHER:

PHONE: CONTACT NAME:

EMAIL: ADDRESS:

DJ/ENTERTAINMENT:

PHONE: CONTACT NAME:

EMAIL: ADDRESS:

HAIR/NAIL SALON:

PHONE: CONTACT NAME:

EMAIL: ADDRESS:

Names & Addresses

MAKE UP ARTIST:

PHONE: CONTACT NAME:

EMAIL: ADDRESS:

RENTALS:

PHONE: CONTACT NAME:

EMAIL: ADDRESS:

HONEYMOON RESORT/HOTEL:

PHONE: CONTACT NAME:

EMAIL: ADDRESS:

TRANSPORTATION SERVICE:

PHONE: CONTACT NAME:

EMAIL: ADDRESS:

Caterer Details

CONTACT INFORMATION:

PHONE: _____

CONTACT NAME: _____

EMAIL: _____

ADDRESS: _____

MENU CHOICE #1:

MENU CHOICE #2:

	YES ✓	NO ✓	COST:
BAR INCLUDED:			
CORKAGE FEE:			
HORS D'OEURS:			
TAXES INCLUDED:			
GRATUITIES INCLUDED:			

Menu Planner

HORS D'OEUVRES

1st COURSE:

2nd COURSE:

3rd COURSE:

4th COURSE:

DESSERT:

Menu Planner

COFFEE/TEA:

FRUIT:

SWEETS TABLE:

WEDDING CAKE:

NOTES:

1 Week Before...

	THINGS TO DO:	NOTES:
MONDAY		
TUESDAY		
WEDNESDAY		
THURSDAY		

REMINDERS & NOTES:

1 Week Before...

	THINGS TO DO:	NOTES:
FRIDAY		
SATURDAY		
SUNDAY		

LEFT TO DO:

REMINDERS: NOTES:

DATE:

DATE:

Wedding Guest List

NAME:	ADDRESS:	# IN PARTY:	RSVP: ✓

Wedding Guest List

NAME:	ADDRESS:	# IN PARTY:	RSVP: ✓

Wedding Guest List

NAME:	ADDRESS:	# IN PARTY:	RSVP: ✓

Wedding Guest List

NAME:	ADDRESS:	# IN PARTY:	RSVP: ✓

Wedding Guest List

NAME:	ADDRESS:	# IN PARTY:	RSVP: ✓

Wedding Guest List

NAME:	ADDRESS:	# IN PARTY:	RSVP: ✓

Wedding Guest List

NAME:	ADDRESS:	# IN PARTY:	RSVP: ✓

Wedding Guest List

NAME:	ADDRESS:	# IN PARTY:	RSVP: ✓

Wedding Guest List

NAME:	ADDRESS:	# IN PARTY:	RSVP: ✓

Wedding Guest List

NAME:	ADDRESS:	# IN PARTY:	RSVP: ✓

Wedding Guest List

NAME:	ADDRESS:	# IN PARTY:	RSVP: ✓

Wedding Guest List

NAME:	ADDRESS:	# IN PARTY:	RSVP: ✓

Wedding Guest List

NAME:	ADDRESS:	# IN PARTY:	RSVP: ✓

Wedding Guest List

NAME:	ADDRESS:	# IN PARTY:	RSVP: ✓

Wedding Guest List

NAME:	ADDRESS:	# IN PARTY:	RSVP: ✓

Wedding Guest List

NAME:	ADDRESS:	# IN PARTY:	RSVP: ✓

Wedding Guest List

NAME:	ADDRESS:	# IN PARTY:	RSVP: ✓

Wedding Guest List

NAME:	ADDRESS:	# IN PARTY:	RSVP: ✓

Wedding Guest List

NAME:	ADDRESS:	# IN PARTY:	RSVP: ✓

Wedding Guest List

NAME:	ADDRESS:	# IN PARTY:	RSVP: ✓

Wedding Guest List

NAME:	ADDRESS:	# IN PARTY:	RSVP: ✓

Wedding Guest List

NAME:	ADDRESS:	# IN PARTY:	RSVP: ✓

Wedding Guest List

NAME:	ADDRESS:	# IN PARTY:	RSVP: ✓

Wedding Guest List

NAME:	ADDRESS:	# IN PARTY:	RSVP: ✓

Wedding Guest List

NAME:	ADDRESS:	# IN PARTY:	RSVP: ✓

Wedding Guest List

NAME:	ADDRESS:	# IN PARTY:	RSVP: ✓

Wedding Guest List

NAME:	ADDRESS:	# IN PARTY:	RSVP: ✓

Wedding Guest List

NAME:	ADDRESS:	# IN PARTY:	RSVP: ✓

Wedding Guest List

NAME:	ADDRESS:	# IN PARTY:	RSVP: ✓

Wedding Guest List

NAME:	ADDRESS:	# IN PARTY:	RSVP: ✓

Wedding Guest List

NAME:	ADDRESS:	# IN PARTY:	RSVP: ✓

Seating Planner

Table #

Table #

Seating Planner

Table #

Table #

Seating Planner

Table #

Table #

Seating Planner

Table #

Table #

Seating Planner

Table #

Table #

Seating Planner

Table #

Table #

Seating Planner

Table #

Table #

Seating Planner

Table #

Table #

Seating Planner

Table #

Table #

Seating Planner

Table #

Table #

Seating Planner

Table #

Table #

Seating Planner

Table #

Table #

Seating Planner

Table #

Table #

Seating Planner

Table #

Table #

Seating Planner

Table #

Table #

Seating Planner

Table #

Table #

Seating Planner

Table #

Table #

Seating Planner

Table #

Table #

Seating Planner

Table #

Table #

Seating Planner

Table #

Table #

Seating Planner

Table #

Table #

Seating Planner

Table #

Table #

Seating Planner

Table #

Table #

Seating Planner

Table #

Table #

Seating Planner

Table #

Table #

Seating Planner

Table #

Table #

Seating Planner

Table #

Table #

Seating Planner

Table #

Table #

Seating Planner

Table #

Table #

Seating Planner

Table #

Table #

Seating Planner

Table #

Table #

Seating Planner

Table #

Table #

Seating Planner

Table #

Table #

Seating Planner

Table #

Table #

Seating Planner

Table #

Table #

Seating Planner

Table #

Table #

Seating Planner

Table #

Table #

Seating Planner

Table #

Table #

Seating Planner

Table #

Table #

Seating Planner

Table #

Table #

Seating Planner

Table #

Table #

Seating Planner

Table #

Table #

Seating Planner

Table #

Table #

Seating Planner

Table #

Table #

Seating Planner

Table #

Table #

Seating Planner

Table #

Table #

Seating Planner

Table #

Table #

Seating Planner

Table #

Table #

Seating Planner

Table #

Table #

Seating Planner

Table #

Table #

Seating Planner

Table #

Table #

Seating Planner

Table #

Table #

Seating Planner

Table #

Table #

Seating Planner

Table #

Table #

Seating Planner

Table #

Table #

Seating Planner

Table #

Table #

Seating Planner

Table #

Table #